Dedicated to my amazing international "Brady Bunch" family.

One Foot in Front of the Other

Poems by
John Rowland

Edited by Lynn Skapyak Harlin
Cover art by Nancy Baum
Photographs by John Rowland

Previous publications of poems contained in this volume
"Echoes" appeared in *Clementine Poetry Journal* in 2015
"Boyhood Summers" appeared in *The Weekly Avocet* in 2018
"A Chill in the Air" appeared in *The Weekly Avocet* in 2019
"September Sunrise on Lake Rousseau" appeared in the quarterly *Avocet Poetry Journal* in 2018
"Summer Afternoon if FL" appeared in *The Weekly Avocet* in 2018
"Dark Times" appeared in *The Blue Collar Review* in 2018
"What Do I Hear" appeared in *The Blue Collar Review* in 2019
"On Anchor" appeared in *Better Than Starbucks* in 2018
"Overnight Passage" appeared in *The Caribbean Compass* in 2015
"Some Other Day" appeared in *Popshot Magazine* in 2016

Published by Hidden Owl, LLC,
Hiddenowl.com

ISBN 978-0-9962371-3-0

Printed in the United States

Contents

Daybreak

When I was five
I awoke at dawn to listen
to birds sing reveille
from the giant mulberry tree
dominating our back yard.

When I was twenty
I awoke at dawn to study
mathematical mysteries from
the previous class before
we went even deeper.

When I was thirty
I awoke at dawn to shower,
dress in appropriate costume,
ride my charger into battle
against demons of the factory.

When I was sixty
I awoke at dawn to discern
the anchor held overnight,
swim naked in the sea
then watch the pelicans
hunt their breakfast.

Now over seventy.
I awake at dawn to welcome
one more day. I think about
all those who've passed on
while I ponder Billy Collins' words.

I Live...

I live in a world demanding answers
to every question ever asked,
a world demanding you take it further
than ever seen in recent past.

I live immersed in Math and Science,
hiding from the unexplained.
Charts and graphs and such contrivance
clearly show us right as rain.

I live within the boundary conditions
where all equations still apply.
I never leave the firm traditions
where everyone is safe and dry.

I wonder how long I can hide here
from all which cannot be explained?
I wonder what it is like out there?
I'll never know if I remain...

Do You Ever Wonder?

Did you ever awaken
thinking, "Where am I?
How did I get here?"

Once a child
now seventy.
When did that happen?

Sixty years ago, no one
could have mapped
my twisted journey.

Serpentine road
littered with
disasters, miracles
mistakes, brilliance
love, hate.
Ending here?

No,
another turn up ahead,
can't see what's beyond.

What if I just stop,
stand and scream
"No Mas"?

What then?
I'll never know
what's beyond
that next turn.

One foot
in front of the other,
the only way I know.

Seems Odd

My compulsion
to dribble ink
into empty space
simply to watch
as it congeals
into words, ideas
then listen
as they're spoken.

I've no need
to raise my voice
above the chorus
riding on the wind.

I need only to
watch those words
appear in smudges
I've left on a page
and hear them
define some specter,
ending its haunting.

I Shall Write a Book

The poem Nancy read described
how a woman, when she became old,
would wear purple in garish combinations.
It occurred to me purple is the color
for Kings, Bishops and, apparently,
Old Women.
I've been none of these.
I shall never wear purple.
I shall write a book instead
with tales of when
I was an athlete, engineer,
teacher, lover, husband,
an explorer, leader, father,
even a frightened little boy
for I was all of these.

I shall write this book
lest I forget
once I was more
than a tired old man.

Blue Crabs and Rivers

Dad bounced the '50 Ford
down the rutted two-track
out to Long Dock
south of the Ferry Yard.
A bucket of chicken guts,
bait for the crab traps,
rattling in the trunk.

Bushels of Blues
Mom in the kitchen
pots boiled, lid knocked off
by giant blue claw
Mom screamed, Dad cussed
big crab tried to get away.

Platters of crabs
filled the sideboard.
Family and friends
filled the dining room.
Beer and penny ante
on Saturday night.
Eight years old,
snug and safe.

Boyhood Summers

Baseball at the park,
all the diamonds filled.
Children's laughter rang.

Today, park quiet,
all the diamonds empty.
Now dust devils rule.

A tranquil blue lake
with lily pads' white flowers,
now a field of mud.

A meadow halved
by a favorite trout stream
now a subdivision.

Treasured images,
no longer realities,
simply memories.

On Mother's Day

Before we are overwhelmed
by waves of pastel sentiment,
we should carefully examine
Motherhood's true nature.

The very steel which keeps your spine erect
was forged in the furnace of her carnal desire.
The twisted helix which defines who you are
fire hardened by her love and determination.

Like the legendary female Grizzly,
Mother taught everything survival requires.
Holding a hostile world at bay
while you grew, while you learned.

Soft pastels? Only vivid colors fly
for the fiercest of Nature's warriors.

Progress

An idea is born.
It will create a better life.
People flock to the banner,
form committees, elect leaders.
Each has their place in the new order.
The organization solidifies
into a monolith
into which people dissolve.
The "better life" becomes slavery
to the organization named
for the forgotten idea.

A Magical Season

A gleam in the eyes of
normally dour accountants,
frantically taping computer keys
forcing printers to spew rainforests
of incomprehensible forms.

There are W2's, 1040EZ's,
all the schedules: A through SE.
Specialized forms for every occasion, like
Orphan Drug Credit, Like Kind Exchanges,
Injured Spouse Allocation,
Unreimbursed Employee Business Expense,
Domestic Production Activities Deduction,
Carbon Dioxide Sequestration Credit,
Depreciation/ Amortization with Known Limitation,
Investment Interest Expense Deduction,
A Look Back Method for Interest computation,
Passive Activity Credit Limitation,
Alternate Motor Vehicle Credit,
and… there seems no end.

A system to serve the legions of minions
charged with collection of over three trillion
to fuel the fiduciary machine of the nation.
Long live the IRS!

Add to the Resume

Spanning a dozen years,
three volumes, leather bound,
written in the Captain's scrawl.
Echoes of adventures, discoveries,
voyages in unfettered freedom.

Sum them together
into a single line
append it to the list
of "Once upon a time…"

What Do I Hear?

I wonder if that rumble
is simply late afternoon
atmospheric instability,
so common in Summer?
Or perhaps…

When last I landed in New York City,
I could swear I saw a tear
on the disenfranchised lady's cheek
while she stood in the harbor
singing from Lazarus' words
inscribed on her tablet.
Perhaps her tears disturb the rest
of those whose vision created a land
where the brave may be free?
Or perhaps…

Within those who still believe in the dream
yet must watch the concept of equality
erode in rivers of hate and fear,
could a festering anger be rumbling
like tectonic forces in conflict?

Whatever the case…

Deep within my bones,
I feel a coming storm.

Dark Times

Panic stricken cop
looks at his gun
as a city burns.
Half-truths obscure
what's been done.

Teenager lies dead,
blood in the street
as a city burns.
Half-truths debate
how he got there.

Vultures circle
feeding on lies.
Spin doctors,
rabble rousers,
making victims
of us all.
Lady Justice smothers
in a blanket of rhetoric.

Echoes of '68 rumble
while raging flames
destroy innocent lives.
The chasm widens.

My country 'tis of thee,
dark tales of anarchy.
Whom can I trust?

In a Moment of Reflection

As I walk, the rain falls softly,
my footprints fill with water.
Every step, the path marked clearly.
I walk. I think. I wonder.

Half a world away, in Jerusalem,
where Jesus' footprints still remain
with those of Mohamed, those of Abraham,
visible, all filled with the blood of children.

Let him without sin cast the first stone…
would he have cast it if he'd known?

Stones beget stones, spears beget spears,
guns beget guns, bombs beget bombs.
Hate propels hate into future years,
a legacy of blood which fills the tombs.

This is the model for the human insanity.
A bullet fired or a stone thrown
provokes a response from fear or vanity,
escalates into death and grief unknown.

Let he who cast the first stone
burn in the eternal fires of Hades,
for he can never hope to atone
for the damage done to future ages.

Cruelty of Myths

We were all raised with them.
We were drilled, brainwashed.
Lies slithered into our minds
wrapped in robes of truth and doctrine.

Vision is clouded, reason blocked,
logic short circuited, judgment twisted.
The lies march like an army
bent on destruction of reality.

September Sunrise on Lake Rosseau

Pines tower over the cottage,
our temporary haven.

Sun paints the shadowed western shore
in mottled red and yellow hues
as it rides its arc to clear the trees.

Amid wisps of mist,
a solitary loon glides
leaving barely a ripple.

An osprey launches off
the east shore rock face,
hailing all with a high-pitched cry.

Wolf tracks in soft sand
forty feet from the porch
near an inverted red canoe.

A whitetail buck steps into view,
assesses the alien in his world.
Steam rises from my coffee cup.

A Winter Sunrise

Snow falls softly:
covers dead fields,
collects on leafless branches,
piles on fence rails,
weaves into needles
of firs, pine, spruce.
Falls among the reeds,
into stands of tall grass.
Penetrates cedars.

Rustling Winter foliage
dampened to a whisper.

Dawn arrives slowly,
cloaked in gray flannel.
Gently, lest it disturb
quiet patches of wood,
caresses the earth
as if a sleeping child.
Casts a muted glow
amid drifting snowflakes.

A Walk in January

A raven's caw in
a late, gray dawn.
City skyline
only shadows.

Cold stones glisten
atop the hill,
awash with the river's
rising mist.

Frigid breeze sweeps in,
dampness penetrates,
my worn joints ache.

If I come this way
on such a day,
even the Sun
will show no mercy.

March in Buffalo

Mounds of plowed snow melt,
becoming piles of grimy soot
beneath oppressive, gunmetal skies.

Lifeless matted brown foliage
oppressed by frigid west winds
littered with winter's trash.

Muddy runoff streams deposit
ankle deep silt layers
across walkways, roadways.

Billowing black clouds deliver
icy spring torrents, transforming
fields into muddy oceans.

Only true believers
maintain expectation
of coming restoration.

Fair Winds, Roy

All living things must die
thus, my day will come.

I have lived as a wild thing,
as free as any creature on this earth,
plying the oceans with dolphins and turtles.

I will die as a wild thing,
without regret or remorse.

It matters little
who mourns my passing
nor what words are said
on my behalf.
The one who created me,
God of the Wild Things,
will bring me home.

In fond memory of Roy Broughton, a true "Old Salt" if there ever was one.

20

Overnight Passage

Glistening droplets fall from the chain
as we release the boat from bondage.
Fresh breeze fills the sails,
hull cuts through the sea,
truly underway.

Ritual begins two hours out.
Sun retires,
sky ignites in reds and golds,
spectacular exit with
a promise of tomorrow.

Night sky fills with stars,
fellow travelers so far away
they could be merely ghosts of
worlds vanished in some past age.
The Southern Cross confirms our course.

A full moon rises,
bathes the sea in pale yellow.
Moonbeam twinkles
mark our path
by dancing in our wake.

At the first rays of the new day
the stars retreat into the coming night.
The Sun reclaims the sky.
Grenada materializes on the horizon,
offering new adventures.

The Open Sea

Fifteen knots
across the beam
yields a steady seven
down the rhumb line.
A gentle six-foot sea
follows under a crystal sky.
Occasional white caps
dot the azure plain
horizon to horizon.
No other ship
nor any island
provides perspective
or mitigates my insignificance.

On land
I convince myself
I am the Master
of all I imagine.
In the open sea
I cannot hide the truth,
not even from my ego.
My puny boat,
my simple skills
inadequate.
My only protection
the benevolent power
of the Universe
allowing me to savor
this sacred moment,
bathing in my irrelevance.

At Anchor

First rays of the sun,
slipping over the east ridge,
dance on indigo.

A new day begins
in the safety of this bay,
this ancient refuge.

A broad open bay,
ringed by lush, rugged hills,
rocky shores, save one.

The sun runs its arc,
indigo turns to azure,
fifty hulls gleaming.

The squall lines pass south,
marching from the Atlantic
bound for Mexico.

Beyond the west ridge
towering thunderheads rise
white against the blue.

The afternoon sun
falls toward the horizon.
Clouds are rose and gray.

The sun sinks away,
azure turns to indigo,
stars light up the sky.

Fifty boats at rest,
guarded by the Canis Major.
The cycle runs on.

The Season

Summer beasts, spawn of
desert-jungle interface,
prowl the trade wind routes.

Warm ocean waters
enable the roaming storms'
journey of terror.

Hunting east to west,
seeking only destruction,
devoid of mercy.

Their names are legends.
Matthew, Maria, Irma,
scrawled in human blood.

Harbingers of death.
Even the bravest hearts fear
the name "Hurricane".

Memories of Felix

Not a ripple, not a whisper,
the lagoon is flat.
The gray green surface
reflects the darkening sky.
Decks cleared,
sails, lines, hatches
all well secured.
Scope at nine to one,
second anchor at the ready.
I cower in the cockpit.
The sun has retreated
beyond the channel.
The rest of us wait,
thirty boats, thirty crews.

It comes out of the darkness.
At first a breeze and a drizzle,
grows to twenty knots
driving heavy rain.
Thickening gloom descends.
Twenty knots to thirty-five,
rain in blinding sheets
bombards the empty decks.
Banshee gusts spring from the dark.
Lagoon, whipped into froth,
blends with the horizontal torrents,
water's surface disappears.

Boat suspended
in malevolent chaos.
Direction meaningless,
lost in enveloping din.
Anchor chain groans,
rigging whines,
hulls roll to hypnotic songs,
fear drives me
to the edge of panic,
exhausted, cold, confused.

Dawn arrives timidly
as the storm moves off,
gaining strength
on a westward quest
to become
some other
sailor's nightmare.

The Visitors

Martinique to stern,
St. Lucia off the bow,
each a shadow on the horizon.
Close reach into eighteen knots,
an eight foot chop
quartered off the port bow,
corkscrew motion relentless.
Hardly the forecast weather.

The first surfaced to the starboard side.
An arching jump announced its presence.
The rest arrived in twos and threes,
numbering more than twenty in all,
eager to showcase their skills.
In the eye level waves quartering to port
sleek gray shapes appeared then dove
reappearing on the starboard side.
There were somersaults, backflips,
tail walks, grand arching jumps,
swimming upside down with
bellies rubbing the bow,
all the while a silly grin.
For half an hour, to our delight,
our fellow mariners entertained.

Abruptly, by unseen signal,
they gathered at the stern
then vanished into the depths.

We were alone again on the open sea,
grinning like our visitors.

Derelicts

In every harbor,
hulls on the beach,
stripped and bleaching.
A mast or a bowsprit
protruding from the water.
A mast less hull
on an encrusted chain.

In every yard,
faded gel coat, rusted stainless,
ragged sails on a broken boom,
sagging rigging, tattered flags.
Forlorn on the jack stands,
waiting.

In every bar,
beer at oh nine hundred,
eyes lifeless, shoulders sloped,
spinning sea stories
while no one listens.
Alone.

These are the debris,
flotsam of sunken dreams.

When I see them I pray,
"Please God, not me."

Autumn Colors

When Fall breezes blow
I miss the autumn colors
here in Florida.

Red, orange and gold
mirrored on the lake's surface
merely memories.

A Scar

My first poem published in a real journal
on the shelf at Barnes and Noble, no less.

Twelve copies on my desk,
where shall I send them?

In a forgotten memory,
a raspy voice speaks,
"What will you do
after graduation, Rowland,
join the Army?
You're not fit for university."
My Honors English Teacher,
the Kerouac wannabe,
four weeks before graduation.

I summoned the great god Google,
set him on a search for my nemesis.
That bastard should get a copy.
Alas, the great Google failed me.
No address found, only an obituary.
I'm just one year too late.

Transformations

Yesterday was once a Tomorrow,
a roiling cloud of expectation,
trepidation or, perhaps,
wild anticipation.
Today Yesterday has become
a note in a journal
or an item on page twelve.

Today might be filled with glory,
fame or crushing failure
or even lust and passion.
Just for Today.

Tomorrow, Time will transform Today
into a footnote on some obscure page
or an inscription on a gravestone
in a dreary glen in a cold winter rain.

Some shimmering crystals on the beach
were once unscalable peaks
in some forgotten Yesterday.

Lake Walton

After all those years, I remember,
out Rt 52 to the weathered
wooden sign on the left.
A gravel track through the brush
opening up to
a dreary field of mud?

From my memory's drawer
I extract images:
a grove of birch next to a tranquil lake,
lily pads with white flowers,
a six-year-old boy rowing
under patient, fatherly direction.
A dozen fresh caught fish
cooked on an open fire,
platter in the center,
table loaded with picnic bounty,
laughter and conversation.
One of many summer Sundays.

Carefully, I replace the images,
close and lock the drawer
lest they become contaminated.

Some Other Day

Somewhere, in a quiet place,
on some other day, in some other year,
I'll learn what I need to know.
I'll see the fear for the lie it is
and let my spirit slip the lines,
set sail on a course newly charted,
a course only I may follow.

Those who remain here will remember
bits and pieces they still hold.
They'll paint a picture or frame a photo
believing they knew me through and through.
But the real me will be in the wind,
leaving only shadows and ripples behind.
History will, as always, be incomplete,
images captured in the twilight,
details hidden by the approaching night.

The Elder

The skull of a man
four hundred thousand years old
captivated me.

Two empty sockets,
portals to an astounding
human adventure.

Tales of nomadic
treks across southern Europe,
camping at seaside.

Hunting elephants
using spears with points hardened
by magic of fire.

Butchering the beasts
with a jagged piece of stone,
his own invention.

A tribe living
beneath a starlit sky, yet
not the sky I know.

Journeying across
tectonic plates differently
arranged from today.

Ancient explorer
leading his brave clan across
a primeval Earth.

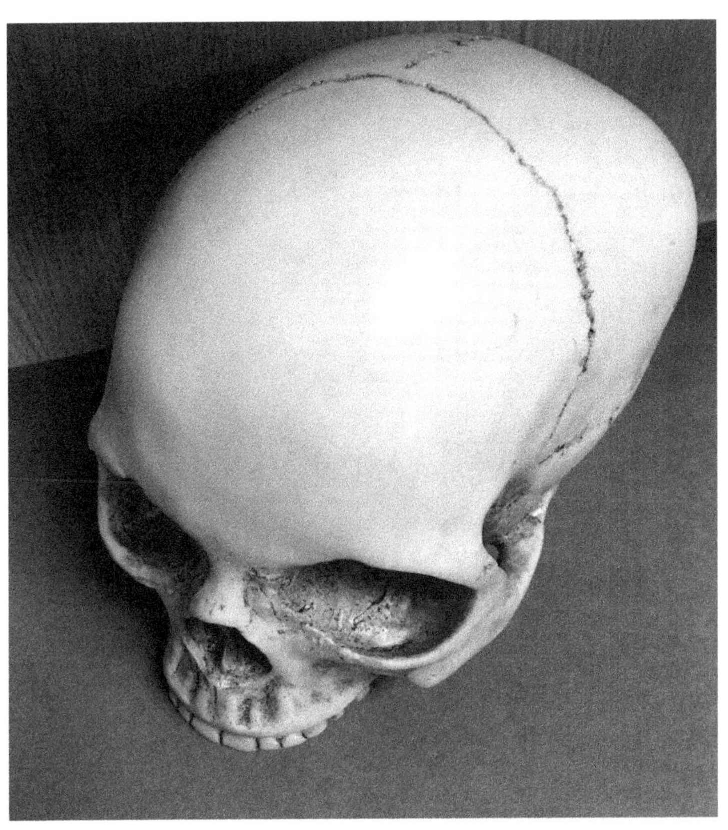

Awakening

Magnolia flowers
appear overnight, vivid
against brown branches.
So delicate, so fragile,
sure victim of coming rain.

Yellow daffodils
in regimental ranks
across the green fields,
Honor Guard to the season
of natural resurrection.

Crimson hibiscus,
afire in the noonday sun,
heralds in rebirth.
Notes of majestic fanfare
resonate from the flower.

Bella de Noche's
fragrance permeates the air.
Bathed in moonlight,
arousing all the senses,
promising things romantic.

Summer Afternoon in Florida

I sit outside
in late afternoon, listening
for the telltale sounds.

Out in the distance,
billowing cauldrons forming
on the horizon.

Soon, low rumblings
bellow across the landscape.
Fresh wind gusts arrive.

The birds go quiet,
fly off to sheltered havens
before storms arrive.

Towering giants hurl
spears of lightning earthward
with resounding crack.

Giant raindrops bombard,
beating a staccato rhythm
on roofs, windowpanes.

Thirsty Earth absorbs
then saturates. Torrents whisk
off mud and debris

Unpacking the Last Box

Among my sweatshirts and jeans,
a bag of orphaned socks.
Dumped on the bed
next to freshly laundered ones.
The ritual of finding matches.
Familiar task softens the edges
of unfamiliar surroundings.

Task completed.
Orphans remain orphans:
gray one with the black stripe,
blue argyle, charcoal pinstripe,
all years unmatched.
Did I think lost mates
would come out of hiding,
follow on their own?
Why cling to these odd scraps?
Orphans back in the bag,
into the trash
with any ghosts
who cling to them.
What other useless burdens
hitchhiked here?

The Bride

In a borrowed white dress
    under Grandmother's fur wrap
        pale blue eye shadow and new spike heels,
            the bubbly little girl I remember is
                the spectacular woman on her father's arm
                    walking the aisle eager to create
                        another branch of our family tree.

4 A. M.

A train announces
its journey through the city.
A boat bellows
its position in the mist.
Too soon the roadways will fill.
Now will become yesterday,
one day closer to
three score and ten,
consumed, gone forever.
An ambulance siren
shatters the quiet.
So much to do, yet
what should be next,
lest tomorrow become
the last yesterday?

A Message

Sleeping fitfully in our new apartment,
from somewhere in the light of the waxing moon,
"Who, o, whooo," startled me awake.
"Who, o, whooo," the call repeated,
clearly calling to me.
Out the door to investigate.

Neighborhood bathed in mottled shadows,
darkened houses behind ancient oaks,
"Who, o, whooo," from the oak next door.
"Who, who," a reply from down the block.
Calls meant for me or just each other?

Legends of Native and Celtic lore,
Denizens of Darkness, Harbingers of Death,
message carriers from beyond?

Playing my light among the branches,
I found a solid shape. With a rush of air,
powerful wings propelled the specter east,
calling "Who, o, whooo," as it soared.

The fabled Messenger of Death
spoke directly to me.
But if Death is merely Change,
perhaps a simple welcome?

Like Any Morning

Her soft, rhythmic breathing
my first recognition
as I awaken.
Pale light through the blinds
accents gold and silver
splayed across her pillow.
Warmth radiating from her
wards off Winter's chill
which permeates the room.
So many years
yet I'm not immune,
arousal unavoidable.
I would caress her softly
but best let her sleep.

Soon enough the imp will rise,
she'll giggle, hatch some plot.
Send us off on some adventure.

Time to make the coffee.

I Miss the Wind

I miss the North wind
moaning through
leafless branches
as it drifts snow
against the door.

The ever-present West wind
bringing capricious weather
across Lake Michigan,
Ontario or Erie.

Most of all, the Trades
singing through the rigging
at anchor in the islands
beneath Orion's watchful eye.

Here, in my lovely home
among the live oaks,
wind only comes darkly
in predatory storms.

Not This Year

I refuse to march with the cliché army
vowing to lose the twenty pounds
they vowed to lose the year before,
same twenty lost in 2013
only to be found in 2014.

I refuse to wear a Fitbit®
reminding me I must walk
fifteen thousand steps per day,
scolding me if I don't.

I refuse to list my faults
carried along these many years,
woven into my fabric.
This year I will not do battle
with my very nature
only to lose to the man I really am.

A Chill in the Air

I recall how children's laughter
carries on crystalline Winter air.
Riding sleds, building snowmen,
snowball fights from fort to fort.
I can hear my laughter,
my children's, my grandchildren's
echoing through time and space.

Now, living far to the south,
I try to hide from Winter
but the cold and damp still find me.
As a chill mist rolls in off the river
my bones ache, my joints creak yet
the soft wool sweater beneath my jacket
carries memories of other Decembers.
The ringing echoes warm my soul.

Echoes

It's late, guests and family gone.
The lights from the tree reflect
in the amber liquid of my glass.
All is quiet, save the echoes.

The sound of children's laughter,
voices of the adults they've become
and of those who shared the empty chair;
all resonate in the empty room.

Ordinary people, sustaining each other.
Each laying one more block
in the ever-stronger castle wall
behind which the new arrive.

My voice will join the echoes
of the Legion of the Ordinary.
Those whom history will never know,
yet upon whose backs the load is carried.

Distorted Reflection in a Murky Pond

An oval, serving plate sized rock
at the roadside, in the sunshine,
lifted slowly as if on hydraulics.
Triangular head appeared to forward.
Barbed tail appeared to aft.
The old one began to toddle
across the macadam road.
First the forward starboard leg
with the aft port side leg
then the pair on opposite corners.
A slow, tenacious pace.
Wary eyes in the wrinkled head
vigilant, detecting any threat.

As the ranger approached, movement stopped.
Head and appendages disappeared.
"Be careful with this guy," ranger warned.
He placed his stick in front of the rock.
A lightning strike of powerful jaws
left stick's end a mass of splinters.
We backed away, the rock came to life,
continued his determined journey.
Finally, he slipped through the ditch
into the murky pond beyond.

His instinctive behavior seemed eerily familiar.

The Tiger

Soundlessly, he moves like a specter.
Invisible, colors blending with the shadows,
wary, piercing eyes, patient demeanor.
He waits, he watches, he follows.

The unwary will know his quickness.
Those who stumble will vanish into darkness.
The weak and the sick will fall to the voracious
appetite, the bottomless abyss.

Sometimes, in the quiet, I feel his presence.
I hear a breaking twig, a crushing leaf.
A movement in the shadows wakens my senses.
I feel his power, awesome past belief.

I know he'll take me, in the end.
He is the predator supreme.
With his power, my will he'll bend.
His claws will flash, his eyes will gleam.

He will win, his name is Time.
But not today, today is mine.

About the Author

John Rowland is a free-lance writer and poet. His work has appeared in *The Caribbean Compass, All at Sea, Clementine Poetry Journal, Popshot Magazine, Better than Starbucks, The Blue Collar Review* and *The Avocet.* His first chapbook, *Hanging Around the Planet,* was published in April of 2013.

After retiring from corporate life in the automotive industry in 2005, John and artist wife, Nancy Baum, took their sloop *S/V Silver Seas* into the Eastern Caribbean. For twelve years they cruised the waters from the Virgin Islands to Trinidad/ Tobago. In 2012, John and Nancy published an e-book, *Eluding the Tiger,* describing some of their experiences during their Caribbean sailing adventure.

John and Nancy now reside in Jacksonville, Florida.